Serial

Killers

A Chilling Collection Of Some
Of The Worlds Most Psychotic
Serial Killers Cases: What
Drove Them To Kill?

Seth Balfour

Seth Balfour

Table of Contents

Introduction   vii
Chapter 1: Jeffrey Dahmer   1
Chapter 2: Gary Ridgway   9
Chapter 3: Fred and Rose West   21
Chapter 4: Donald Harvey   31
Chapter 5: Dennis Nilsen   41
Chapter 6: Donald "Pee Wee" Gaskins   50
Chapter 7: Dr. Harold Frederick Shipman   59
Chapter 8: Pedro Alonso Lopez   64
Conclusion   70

Want more books?

Would you love books delivered straight to your inbox every week?

Free?

How about non-fiction books on all kinds of subjects?

We send out e-books to our loyal subscribers every week to download and enjoy!

All you have to do is join! It's so easy!

Just visit the link at the end of this book to sign up and then wait for your books to arrive!

Introduction

Killing brings grief to anyone, especially to the family and friends of the victims. Sometimes, out of self preservation, one can be forced to kill someone to protect themselves. At times, it could be anger or revenge that can drive a person to murder an individual who wronged them. If not those, then perhaps, it is ambition.

What could possibly be inside the minds of these people who experience euphoria in murdering innocent lives? Did something happen in their childhood? Did an accident shake their sanity? Was it control? Whatever it is, hearing the true stories of serial killers will make you feel more cautious in your own environment. Is your doctor as caring as you perceive him to be? The couple living down the street, are they innocent?

In this book, you will learn about 6 people who took pleasure in raping, killing and torturing innocent people... how did they do it? Why did they do it?

Thanks again for purchasing this book, I hope you enjoy it!

Chapter 1: Jeffrey Dahmer

Emotion: this is sometimes what causes people to commit a crime. Another term for this is Crime of Passion. But what would drive a man to sexually offend and kill 17 people in the span of 13 years? Let's look at the mind of Jeffrey Dahmer.

Jeffrey was born on May 21, 1960 in Milwaukee, Wisconsin. He had loving parents named Lionel and Joyce Dahmer-- both gave him everything a child could ask for. Growing up, Jeffrey was a cheerful boy, until he reached the age of 6 when he had to undergo surgery because of his double hernia.

Shortly after his operation, his mother gave birth to his younger brother. The surgery and the birth of his brother marked Jeffrey's change in attitude. From a cheery disposition, he became insecure. When they had to move to Iowa due to his father's work, his insecurities took a turn for the worse. He became a withdrawn teenager with virtually no friends.

Thinking carefully, you might say that Jeffrey's condition was not unheard of. There have been many children and teenagers who grew up to be disengaged, but not all of them became serial killers. Sure they were often misunderstood, but through time, they would find their "zone" and would be able to live a functional and satisfying life. So what went wrong in Jeffrey's case?

Shortly after graduation from high school, Jeffrey had his first victim...

Steven Hicks was a simple (and perhaps gay) hitchhiker. In June of 1978, Steven was picked up by Jeffrey. They went straight to Lionel and Joyce's house, got drunk, and had sex. When Steven attempted to leave, Jeffrey killed him by blowing a barbell on his head. After that, he dismembered the corpse and packed the different body parts in plastic bags and then hid the bags in the woods at the back of the house.

Around the time of his first killing, he became an alcoholic, but at his age, it was common. After all, being 18 signified legal freedom. He enrolled in Ohio State University, but after just one term, he was kicked out due to his heavy drinking. By that time, his parents were already divorced and his father just recently re-married.

The drinking problem got so out of proportion that he got kicked out from the army where his father enlisted him to. He stayed in the Armed Forces and posted in Germany for only two years before he was discharged. In his time there, no evidence was found that he killed others.

After his discharge, he went back home to Ohio, went into the woods where he hid Steven's body, got the bags out, and pulverized the dismembered corpse using a hammer. He scattered Steven's pulverized remains further and wider into the woods.

When he was arrested due to disorderly conduct, his father decided that he needed a new environment. Jeffrey was sent to live with his grandmother in Wisconsin. While living there, she became worried because of his strange behaviour, and due to the weird items in his room. First there was a .357 magnum under the bed and a male mannequin in the closet. He was also overly attached to dead animals: often times he would get a dead squirrel, dissect it, and melt the body with chemicals.

In the summer of 1988, his grandmother asked Jeffrey to move out, but unknown to her, he committed his second murder while still in her care.

The second victim was also named Steven-- Steven Toumi. They met in a gay bar, checked in a hotel, drank beer, had sex and when Jeffrey woke up, he saw Steven's dead body beside him. However, he claimed that he couldn't remember if he killed him or not. He purchased a huge suitcase and put the body inside it.

He brought it home to his grandmother's home, transported it to the basement, had sex with it and masturbated over it. In the end, he also dismembered the corpse and threw it in the garbage.

This continued for many years even after he was thrown out of his grandmother's home. Often times, he would pick his victims in gay bars. He was also very careful in picking them: frequently, he made sure that his victims were felons, so that their disappearance would matter to almost no one. Jeffrey promised them money for sex, or payment for posing nude.

While drinking, he would lace their liquor with drugs to make them fall asleep. His most common method of killing was strangling to death before finally having sex with them. At times he also masturbated over them before dismembering the bodies and throwing the body parts in the garbage. There were even instances when he experimented on the bodies: he performed lobotomies, sometimes even when the victims were still alive.

He would inject muriatic acid into their brains just to see if they would survive. Most of them instantly died, but he claimed that one man survived for a few days in a zombie-like state. Later on, he claimed that he did this to know whether he would be able to have a "youthful" and "submissive" sexual partner.

It seemed like Jeffrey wanted to exercise so much control over them. Creepier was the fact that he kept souvenirs-- mostly the victims' skulls or genital areas. He was also known to take photos of the victims: each killing stage had a photo for him to be able to relive the gratifying moments. His neighbors began smelling "something awful" as well as hearing loud falling objects, but they didn't pursue any action against it...

You must be thinking why he wasn't caught. Well, he was eventually. Just not for the gruesome murders, but for molestation. At one point he molested a 13-year old boy and was tried because of it. He pleaded guilty-- saying that the boy appeared to be older than his age. On his trial day in May 1989, he was very "apologetic"-- he said that he saw his mistakes and how the event made him realize that he needed to make changes in his life.

His lawyer argued that what he needed was "help" and not "persecution". Unfortunately, the judge agreed to it. Jeffrey's sentence was imprisonment for 1 year on a "day release" basis. That meant that he could go to work at day, and return to the prison at night.

His father, Lionel, pleaded for a psychological evaluation before releasing him, but he was granted an early release after only 10 months. He returned home to his grandmother's house and stayed there for 3 months. It seemed like he didn't add to the body count during that three-month period, until he transferred to his own apartment in 1990.

Jeffrey's case was almost the perfect crime- aside from his molestation case, he appeared to be an ordinary felon, not a serial killer. In 1991, the police almost had the chance to catch him-- but they took his word because he was a "white man" in a poor African-American town.

On May 26, 1991, Sandra Smith, Jeffrey's neighbor, called the police because a young Asian boy was running naked and scared. Jeffrey showed up, telling the authorities that the Asian guy was his 19-year old lover. He (Asian guy), had just drank too much, hence his strange behavior.

Sandra and her daughter insisted that the boy, named Konerak Sinthasomphone, was terrified of Jeffrey, but the police still took Jeffrey's side. They even escorted them home, clearly not wanting anything to do with a domestic dispute. If only they had inspected the inside of Jeffrey's apartment, they would have seen a decomposing body, along with the "souvenirs" and the photographs of his different victims. When the police left, Jeffrey strangled Konerak to death and proceeded with his rituals.

Although Jeffrey seemed lucky, he was finally caught on July 22, 1991. The supposed victim was Tracy Edwards. He was lured into Jeffrey's apartment and was threatened with a butcher knife, fortunately though, he escaped even when he was handcuffed. He asked for police help and told them about a "weird guy".

When the police arrived at the apartment, Jeffrey even had the "decency" to offer the cuff keys. Tracy told the police that the knife was in the bedroom so the two officers inspected the things there and found the victims' photos. A further search revealed a head in the fridge...

The first officer shouted to his partner to arrest Jeffrey, who fought hard but was eventually subdued. Aside from the pictures and head, three more heads in the refrigerator were found along with dismembered limbs. There were also skulls and preserved genitals contained in jars.

Given the majority of Jeffrey's victims were African American, the case was labelled as discriminatory as well. The police even had to "protect" Jeffrey by placing him in a bullet-proof area. Even though he confessed to the killings, his plea was still not guilty. Later on, he changed his plea to guilty in virtue of insanity.

From there he related the gruesome things that he did

which included necrophilia, sodomy, and cannibalism (yes, it was later confirmed that he also consumed some of his victims' body parts). He said that those things would only be committed by an insane person.

The judge however, sided with the prosecution. For them, Jeffrey was well aware of his evilness but he chose to do them anyway. In the end, he was sentenced to 15 lifetime imprisonment which was equivalent to 957 years in prison.

In prison, Jeffrey appeared to be withdrawn at first, but eventually was included in the activities and worked alongside other jail mates. He even announced himself to be a Born Again Christian. On November 28, 1994, Jeffrey was killed by Christopher Scarver after he (Jeffrey) allegedly provoked him. Scarver also relented that Jeffrey's crimes disturbed him.

Chapter 2: Gary Ridgway

During the 1980s and the 1990s, prostitutes and runaways in Seattle and Tacoma, Washington feared for their lives. Just think about this: 42 women were confirmed dead from 1982 to 1984 – all of them died under the hands of one man: Gary Ridgway.

And from his own lips, the serial killer admitted to killing more, so much that he lost count. The authorities assumed he murdered at least 71 women, many of whom were abducted along the Pacific Highway South and were strangled out of their last breath.

Brutal, but intelligent. The hallmarks of a full-blown, unrepentant murderer.

Authorities figured out that he left most of the bodies in the deep, wooded areas around the Green River, which runs west of the Cascade Mountains. When found, the remains of the victims were often in clusters; many of them turned up nude and posed.

Reports said Gary Ridgway developed a habit of "returning" to the corpses to have sexual intercourse with them. To cover his tracks and confuse the police, Gary also often threw writing materials, thrash, gums, and cigarettes in the dumpsite.

On August 15, 1982, 41-year-old Robert Ainsworth hopped into his raft and traveled down the Green River, towards Seattle's city limit. "Just an ordinary day," he thought, because he had done this trip numerous times before and nothing special came out of it. Well, that day would be different.

As he sailed down the river, he saw two men by the riverbanks– an older, balding one, and a younger fellow beside their pickup. Assuming that they were out fishing, Robert shouted: "Caught any?" To which the man replied: "None!" Soon enough, perhaps because no fish latched on their baits, the two men left in their pickup and Robert was left alone on the river.

That was until his eyes met an unfamiliar, ghostly face, floating, swaying above the currents of the river.

"A black mannequin," Robert thought. He took a pole and tried to fish the "mannequin", but because of the weight, his raft overturned and he fell into the river. That was when he realized that it was a dead body, and, within seconds, he discovered that another corpse was floating – this one was also black and half naked.

Horrified, Robert swam as fast as he could toward the riverbank, sat himself in the area where the pickup was situated just minutes before, and waited for help. Half an hour later, a man with two kids passed by; Robert told them about the nightmarish encounter and pleaded them to call the police.

The officer who arrived was disbelieving, but when he got a good look at the body, he called for backup. After questioning Robert and securing the area, another detective saw a third body, but this one wasn't in the river – it was in the wooded area nearby. Clearly, the young victim – who was later identified as Opal Mills, 16 – was strangled: a pair of blue jeans was knotted around her neck. Bruises were present denoting struggle.

Medical examination revealed that the other two were strangled as well, and they both had pyramid-shaped rocks inserted in their vagina. One of the two victims found in the river was Marcia Chapman, 31, a mother of two who had been missing for two weeks and who was dead for about a week when Robert discovered her. The other was Cynthia Hinds, 17; police estimated that she had been in the river for several days.

The discovery of these three bodies prompted the authorities to look back several days earlier when Deborah Bonner's corpse was found; she was also strangled, like Wendy Lee Coffield (found one month earlier) and her friend, Leanne Wilcox, who was discovered 6 months prior.

Six bodies in a period of six months, and the police knew that there were more. If they didn't catch the killer, the bodies would continue to pile up like used clothes waiting to be laundered.

Because of the obvious presence of a serial killer, the King County's Sheriff Office formed the Green River Task Force, with its most notable members, Robert Keppel (criminal investigator) and David Reichert (detective), who, interestingly, also interviewed Ted Bundy, a prominent serial killer who was already jailed at that time.

Asked what he thought of the Green River Case, Bundy expressed that the murderer had a habit of returning to the corpse (he was right), hence, if the police caught a fresh grave, they must wait.

Despite the tip from a successful murderer, catching Ridgway proved to be a tough task, not because there was little information to begin with, but because there was a lot. The police were swamped with numerous phone calls, tips, evidences, and reports, that everything became impossible to process.

Many of the clues were lost, some got misplaced, and others were overlooked. After some time, the impossibility of the task drove the authorities to enlist help from civilian volunteers.

During the course of the investigation, they found out that most of the victims were either prostitutes or runaways – many knew each other personally and some of them even frequented the same place. This paved the start of the hunt – detectives and uniformed personnel began their investigation in areas that the victims frequented; they asked hundreds of people, mostly prostitutes, but they came up mostly empty handed partially due to the fact that prostitutes didn't trust them.

Fortunately, in 1982, a few of the sex workers spoke up – one of them was Susan Widmark, then only 21 years old.

In her story, Susan was picked up by a middle aged man, in a blue and white pickup truck. Shortly after agreeing to the solicitation, the unnamed man drew out his pistol and brandished it toward her – crushing any chance of escape. The man brought her to a secluded area and then proceeded to violently rape here.

After the act, she was allowed to get dressed, but the pistol was still pointed at her; it was during the second drive that she escaped – she jumped out of the pickup at a stoplight. In her account, Susan said the rapist made a reference to the river killings...

A similar thing happened to Debra Este, who, at that time, was only 15 years old. According to Debra, a man in a blue and white pickup saw her walking on the highway and offered to give her a lift. Thinking nothing of it, she agreed. All of a sudden, the man pointed a pistol in her, forced her to perform oral sex, then handcuffed her and left her in a wooded area.

Thinking that the man in the blue and white pickup was the serial killer they were looking for, the police scouted the area for him. They thought they found the jackpot with a butcher named Charles Clinton Clark who owned a blue and white pickup and who, upon investigation, was found to own two handguns. When shown with Clark's IDs, both Debra and Susan positively identified him as their rapist.

But was he the Green River Killer? The police were skeptical; firstly, Clark's MO involved letting his victims escape. Secondly – and the more important factor – he had solid alibis at the time many of the murders took place. And as if to prove his innocence to the Green River case, one woman disappeared while he was being booked for Susan's and Debra's rape cases.

Mary Bridgett Meehan was more than 8 months pregnant when she disappeared near the Western Six Motel. Interestingly, the motel was one of the areas the prostitutes who fell victim to the hands of the Green River Killer frequented.

Clark wasn't the killer. The authorities knew it, that they were back to ground zero...

As sad as it was, the hunt for Gary Ridgway kept the police busy for almost two decades. In one of his interviews, Ridgway said that he picked prostitutes and runaways for two reasons: first, they were easy to get (hence, easy to kill), and second, the chances of them being reported missing was slim to none (meaning, more chances for him to escape punishment).

In fact, he often took valuables from the victims to prevent authorities from identifying them. As for the clustering of the corpses, the serial killer said he did it for the sole purpose of keeping track of his victims.

The saddest part of the case happened when the police arrested him out of suspicion, then released him due to the lack of evidence. The first time he was arrested was in 1982; in 1983 he became a suspect, and a year after the police asked him to undergo a lie-detector test, which he passed.

By then, the authorities already determined that Ridgway a) had the hobby of picking up prostitutes since he solicited one of the undercover police officers, and b) could hurt a prostitute if he wanted to. This is because back in 1980, he was accused of strangling a prostitute, but plead that it was only a self-defense act since the woman started biting him.

Reluctant to release the man without a fight, Matt Haney, one of the detectives, dug deeper. He found out that in 1982, a police officer stopped Ridgway while he was with Kelly McGinness, who was probably one of the Green River Victims though it wasn't confirmed.

In 1983, Ridgway became a suspect in the disappearance of Marie Malvar – a confirmed victim. Apparently, Marie's boyfriend, pointed Ridgway's house as the last place he had seen his girlfriend in before she went missing.

The most damning discovery, perhaps, was the interview with Ridgway's ex-wife and the people who knew him. First, his ex-wife said he often visited a certain dumpsite; turned out the same dumpsite was where many victims were found.

Secondly, many prostitutes identified him as a man who matched the suspect's description. Third, Ridgway used to pass a strip where many victims were also dumped DAILY on his way to work as a truck painter. And lastly, he was found to have been absent from work on the day one of the victims disappeared.

For these reasons, the police were able to obtain a warrant to search his home in 1987. They found no significant evidence that could tie him to the murders, so he was released from police custody, but not before they obtained "bodily specimens" from him.

Despite the years that passed and the obvious lack of progress, Reichert couldn't let go of the Green River Killings, so on April 2001, he chose to reopen the case – that time, technology was on their side and that time, too, he was already the Sheriff of King County.

He formed a new team, first consisting of only 6 members, but grew to 30 within months. All the evidence was re-examined, samples were sent to labs, and finally, on September 2001, great news almost brought Reichert to his knees. The semen found in some of the victims matched the specimen they took from Ridgway.

On November 30, 2001, Gary Ridgway was arrested yet again, but this time, he wouldn't escape.

Like many serial killers, Gary started out low. His MO started with picking prostitutes up, building rapport by showing them a picture of his son, and then having sex with them. After the intimacy, came the terror. From behind, he would strangle them; at first using his bare hands, but after some time, he found the habit dangerous: the victims would claw their way out, causing him injuries and bruises which he feared would one day make him suspicious.

Since then, he used ligatures. The sites of the murders were anticlimactic: some took place in his house, some in his truck, and the others in whatever secluded area he could find.

But the ultimate question remained unanswered: what drove this man to murder dozens upon dozens of women? Perhaps, we can find an answer in learning about his youth.

Born in 1949, Gary Ridgway was a native of Salt Lake City, Utah, and like many serial killers, his childhood was a troubled one. His mother, according to his neighbors, was a domineering female. At the age of 14, Ridgway still wet his bed and whenever his mother learned of an incident, she would order him to go to the bathroom naked, and there, she would bathe him.

These baths both embarrassed and aroused young Gary, driving him to have sexual fantasies featuring his own mother. As a young child, Ridgway only had an IQ of 82, sealing his fate as the boy who didn't do well in class. His former classmates said he was quiet and "largely forgettable."

When Ridgway was 16, he lured a 6-year old boy into the woods and stabbed him in the stomach, damaging the liver; fortunately though, the little boy survived. According to both their accounts, Ridgway left the scene happy and laughing, all the while saying: "I always wondered what it would be like to kill someone..."

After he graduated high school from Tyee High School at the age of 20, he married 19-year-old Claudia Kraig. Despite being a new husband, Ridgway chose to join the Navy and serve in a supply ship; there, he had multiple sexual relationships with prostitutes to the point of acquiring gonorrhea, which angered him to no end but didn't stop him from soliciting the sexual workers. Back at home, Claudia also had extra-marital affair, hence, their marriage ended just within a year.

His ways with prostitutes didn't change even after marrying his second wife, Marcia Winslow, who reported that during their marriage, Ridgway became very religious. He would read the Bible at home and at work, he would visit their neighbors to spread the word of God, and often times, he would cry after a sermon.

Winslow also accounted on how insatiable her ex-husband was, demanding sex several times a day, in unconventional positions, and at the weirdest of places (including public ones). In the end, the two also ended their relationship in divorce.

In 1988, Ridgway married his third wife, Judith Mawson, who had no idea about the gruesome crimes her partner had committed until the police contacted her in the year of the arrest. When asked about the behavior of her husband, Mawson relented that, sometimes, Ridgway would go to work very early, though he claimed that it was for overtime pay. She also remembered that his house had no carpet – the police said he probably used it to wrap one of the bodies.

Ridgway admitted that his murders dwindled down after he married Mawson because he truly loved her. "I feel like I have saved lives by keeping him happy," Mawson (now Lynch) once said in an interview.

The death penalty was the original punishment for Ridgway, but as it was, he struck a deal: he would admit to 48 murders and cooperate with the investigation to the best of his ability in exchange of his life. When people learned of this deal, they were outraged, especially the family of the victims.

For them, it was clear that Ridgway should die, for if he didn't, then it might signal the end of the death penalty in Washington. The people thought: if a man who killed 48 women in just two years escaped the death penalty, then what crime is punishable by death?

In the end, the deal pushed through and Ridgway got 48 life sentences with no possibility of parole. On top of the 48 life sentences which should be served consecutively, the judge added another 480 years for tampering with the evidences – 10 years each for his victim.

Exactly how many victims he had, no one knows for certain. But one could not believe the claim that he stopped killing for so many years. Serial killers can slow down, especially if there is a heightened activity on the side of the law, but they never truly stop. Gary fit right into the profile of a serial killer –

- he had a difficult childhood
- had a low IQ
- developed a love-hate relationship with his mother
- gained a voracious sexual appetite
- his victims belonged to a certain group (women, either prostitutes or runaways)
- his MO had patterns (pickup, rape, strangle, dump in clusters, and revisit)

So did he stop, or did his victims reach more than a hundred? The idea is not far-fetched: Ridgway once admitted that he saw prostitutes are disposable objects, so it didn't truly matter if he killed them.

*Note: it was later found out that Ridgway failed the lie-detector test he took in 1984. Because of this the FBI imposed a stricter rule in examining the results.

Chapter 3: Fred and Rose West

Till death, do us part. This is a common vow during a wedding ceremony. It is also preceded with other sweet promises like in sickness and in health, and for richer or poorer. But somewhere in those vows, Fred and Rose West added a horrifying promise: To kill together, even taking the lives of their own daughters.

Before we begin dissecting their crimes, let us first have a look at their lives while they were growing up.

Frederick "Fred" West was born to Walter and Daisy West on September 29, 1941. Unlike the case of Jeffrey Dahmer, Fred grew up in an unfit environment. There were 6 West children in total and Fred was the second born. According to reports, he was said to be their mother's favorite, but later it was suspected that his mother was sexually abusing him while growing up.

Fred never mentioned this, but he did report that his father was having a sexual relationship with his sisters. It's as if incest was a common practice in the West family. That account of his, however, was not proven.

To make matters worse, Fred was considered an unattractive boy. He also didn't do well in school. The situation was so dire that he had to drop out at the age of

15 even though he was almost illiterate. When he reached the age of 16, his looks improved and he became more popular with girls. However, at 17, he encountered a terrible vehicular accident.

The accident resulted in him being in a comatose for 1 week and a metal plate had to be implanted in his head. On top of that, the accident broke his leg- the damage was so severe that his leg became shorter than the other. After only two years, his head endured yet more damage when a girl pushed him down from the fire escape of a pub. Apparently, Fred was "feeling up" the girl under her skirt.

Could it really be his head injuries that brought him to become a serial killer? According to accounts, after the two accidents, Fred became known for his petty crimes. These petty crimes though, took a turn for the worse. When he was 19, he was accused of impregnating a 13 year old girl.

He didn't serve any time in a correctional facility because his doctor said he suffered from fits of epilepsy, but his family sent him to one of his sisters. Even with this action, it was clear that his family disowned him.

While away, he reunited with his ex-lover Rena Costello. Rena, too, was known for theft and involvement in prostitution. At that time, Rena was carrying another man's child whose father was a Pakistani. They made others believe that the child, whom they named Charmaine, was adopted, just so they could explain why she was of Asian descent.

While together, Fred always demanded sex with Rena, but the sex he was looking for was "not regular". By then he was already working as an ice cream truck driver which gave him access to other non-suspecting girls.

Soon enough in 1964, they had their own daughter which they named Anne Marie. After Fred accidentally ran over a 4 year old boy with his truck, Rena left him with the girls, along with Anna McFall which was her friend. Fred, Anna, and the two girls (Anne Marie and Charmaine), went home to Gloucester where Fred worked in a slaughterhouse.

Many believed that his work there served as the catalyst for his killing desires. Anna and Fred began a relationship and when Anna became pregnant, she demanded that he should divorce Rena, but instead of giving into her request, Fred killed her, dismembered her body, and buried it somewhere. A few months later, Rena also divorced him.

When Fred landed a job as a bakery truck driver, he met

his wife and accomplice to crimes, Rosemary Letts.

Rosemary "Rose" West was originally Rosemary Letts, daughter to Daisy and Bill Letts. From the start, Rose's birth was clouded with violence. Rose was born in Devon, England on November 29, 1953. While Daisy was pregnant with her, she was under the state of severe depression. Since there were still no medications available to treat her condition, they opted for her to undergo ECT or electro-convulsive therapy. The ECT might have caused injury to Rose; hence, while she was growing up, she performed very poorly at school.

On top of not being bright, Rose was also overweight. She was often bullied and she responded by attacking the bullies physically. Her parents also did not share a harmonious relationship. Often times, her father would punish them for small faults. It was also reported that Bill was sexually harassing her.

When she reached her teens, she became sexually aggressive. She was caught sexually fondling her younger brother but wasn't punished for it. Due to her father's strictness, Rose began having relationships with older men. When she reached the age of 15, Daisy was finally done with Bill's violent nature.

They moved out and lived with Rose's older sister and her husband. Due to this, Rose garnered more freedom when it came to her sexual desires with different men. So imagine the family's shock when she decided to move back in with her father.

Around the time of her return to Bill's care, she met her future husband, Fred West. Not surprisingly, Bill did not approve of their relationship, especially since Fred was 12 years older than Rose. Bill went to their trailer home and threatened Fred, but to no avail. The unhealthy relationship between Fred and Rose continued.

When Fred was sent to jail due to some petty crimes, Rose was left in the house to take care of all the children: Charmaine, Anne Marie, and Heather-- her and Fred's own daughter. Naturally, she didn't like taking care of her step daughters, but no one would suspect her of being capable of murdering one of them.

Well, she was.

In 1971, Rose killed Charmaine. Upon Fred's return from prison, the two of them hid the body, but not before Fred chopped off Charmaine's toes and fingers first. When Rena (Fred's first wife) went to them to see Charmaine, she also disappeared. It was later discovered that she was strangled to death before Fred and Rose dismembered her toes and fingers.

As if nothing happened, the two married each other in 1972. In the same year, Rose gave birth to their second daughter whom they named Mae. Now a family of five, they moved to a larger home; No. 25 Cromwell Street. There, they were able to take lodgers to help with the rent.

The life of the family was "creepy" to say the least. First, even though they were married, Fred encouraged Rose to enter prostitution both for money and for fun. Rose, also welcomed this suggestion. Fred even watched Rose's sexual encounters-- he also took photos of her.

When the two of them were having sex, their tastes were unconventional. Fred too, had sideline sexual encounters: most of them were with underage girls. The cellar of their home was turned into a torture zone-- the first victim was Fred's daughter Anne Marie, who was only 8 years old at that time. Rose would hold Anne Marie down and Fred would then rape her. The poor girl was threatened by her supposed parents: if she so much as talked about what happened, she would be killed.

With their sexual activities, it was not surprising that Rose gave birth to seven more children. Fred fathered three of them, one could have been with Bill (it was confirmed that Bill and Rose continued to have an incestuous relationship even after Rose gave birth to her 4th child), and the rest were fathered by Rose's customers in prostitution.

Aside from sexual adventures, the couple did not engage in any more killings and seldom did they take unwilling victims (except for Anne Marie). The adventures though were extended to non-family members when the then 17 year old Caroline Owens fell victim to their deeds.

Carolyn was hired by the couple to be their nanny, but when she was stripped, tortured, and raped, she went straight to the police even after all the threats from the Wests. The authorities however sided with Fred as he said that Carolyn was a willing partner.

The children in the West household were all controlled. They were not to speak of the going-ons inside the house. Fed up with everything, Anne Marie moved out and lived with her boyfriend. This didn't stop Fred in Molesting the younger Heather and Mae.

While Mae relented to his father's activities, Heather resisted. In 1986 though, she made the mistake of telling one of her friends about what was happening in their home. Fred and Rose murdered her, and buried her body in the back garden. Of course, they also removed her toes and fingers. Stephen, their son, was also asked to assist in the "burial".

After this, many new victims emerged. First was Lynda Gough, she was a seamstress who knew the couple in person. Then came Carol Ann Cooper, who was innocently walking home after watching a movie in a theater. Lucy Katherine Partington was another of their victims-- she was abducted by the couple, tortured and raped for one whole week, before finally being murdered. After them, 5 more women were murdered by the Wests.

All of the bodies of the victims were buried either under the garage or in the garden. Since burying the bodies would garner a lot of attention, they made it seem like they were doing home improvements. To afford the materials needed, Fred had to steal and loot. Although their actions were suspicious, none of the neighbors thought about murders.

When May 1992 came, they were finally caught, but not for murder. Fred recorded a video of himself while raping one of his daughters. When said daughter told her friends about it, one of them reported the Wests. The investigator, Hazel Savage, waited until another victim emerged before preparing the search warrant on the house.

The warrant was simply for evidence of child abuse, but upon Hazel's search, the police found so much more. They arrested Fred for rape (no murders were found) and Rose was announced as an accomplice. The children were put into state custody.

Rose became depressed after the arrest, so much that she even attempted suicide. Fortunately, one of her sons stopped her. The shocking part of the case was when the victims retracted their claims. Even through their backing out, Hazel Savage continued her investigation.

For her, something was very wrong, especially since she knew Fred from his relationship with Rena. Hazel also thought that Heather's sudden disappearance was suspicious, and her interviews with the children seemed to be "controlled". Finally, she was able to obtain another warrant.

After that, Fred confessed to the murders-- telling the police that it was only his doing so as to protect Rose. However, Fred refused to admit that he raped any of the victims. He reported that they were all willing to have sex with him.

Rose tried to wash her hands of all the things that happened so she distanced herself from her husband, even to the point of telling the police that she was also a victim. The police didn't fall for her tricks though, so she was still tried for both rape and murder. The problem was, all the evidence that pinned her down was circumstantial.

Good thing Janet Leach gave her statement. Janet Leach was Fred's "appropriate adult" - in simpler terms, his guardian. She said that Fred told her about Rose's murders. In the end, On November 22, 1995, Rose was sentenced for lifetime imprisonment for 10 counts of murder.

Fred's verdict was given earlier, on December 13, 1994. He was charged for 12 counts of murder, but on the New Year of the following year, he hanged himself using bedsheets. His funeral was unattended, except for 5 of his kids.

Their home at No. 25 Cromwell Street was demolished and was turned into a pathway in 1996.

Chapter 4: Donald Harvey

Working in a hospital is a rewarding job – you get to see patients healing, you experience their transition from dependency to autonomy, and at the end of the day, you could tell yourself that you helped them get better.

The other side of the coin is tragic: some diseases have no cure, several cases are hopeless, and you can practically feel the determination leave your patients' eyes. Getting attached to them is sometimes inevitable, hence, in whatever way you could, you could lighten things up for them.

Some people, however, use this attachment as an excuse to feed on their desire to kill. Donald Harvey was one of them. From 1970 to 1987, he was able to "help"36-57 people get out of their misery by cutting their lives short. The murders sealed his title as "The Angel of Death".

Born in April 15, 1952, Donald "That Old Plymouth Boy" Harvey was brought up with love and affection – at least that was what his father said. He was a native of Butler County, Ohio, but shortly after his birth, they moved to Booneville, Kentucky, in Cumberland Plateau, a part of the Appalachian Mountains.

Harvey, during his school days, was one of the teachers' favorites. Smart and introverted, he appeared to be the silent one who would one day rule. In fact, the elementary school principal, David Andrews, clearly remembered how pleasing Donald's personality was: he always had a

Seth Balfour

smile to offer, he came to school well-dressed, and would speak with politeness. Nothing out-of-the-ordinary permeated from him.

Kids his age, however, saw him as a loner who preferred the company of books and adults. In reports, it was said to be because he found school boring – as if learning from children his age was without a challenge. At Booneville High School, he easily obtained A's and B's, and soon enough thought all the studying was pointless. He dropped out of high school, but he obtained his GED at the age of 17.

It is often said that too much intelligence leads to lack of compassion, but it could not be ascertained whether this "school boredom" had anything to do with his killing spree.

What could have affected his violence was the abuse he suffered from his uncle and another male neighbor: reports said that Harvey was sexually abused by these two males from the age of four and it went on for a couple of years.

Out of school and without a job, Harvey moved to Cincinnati, Ohio to care for his ailing grandfather in Marymount Hospital. In doing so, he became a familiar face in the institution that he was offered a job as an orderly. Unfortunately, Harvey accepted the offer, and, in just two weeks, he became the Angel of Death who would go unnoticed for many years.

Harvey's original duties range from dispensing medications, inserting and removing catheters, to attending to other medical needs; in other words, he was handed the job that would urge him to spend as much time as he could with the patients.

While others would thrive in the job, thinking that they were doing a noble thing, Harvey merely thought that, as an orderly, he had the right to rule over someone else's life: he could spare patients, or he could kill them.

On May 30, 1970, Harvey was having an ordinary shift; everything was okay, it was uneventful... until he went into Logan Evans' room. Evans was a stroke patient, but Harvey didn't care, he still killed him without remorse. According to reports, he went to Evans' room to help him, but upon arrival, the patient started to rub feces in Harvey's face.

Angered by the action, the next thing the orderly realized was that he was smothering the patient with plastic and a pillow until he died. After the murder, he cleaned the patient, hopped into the shower, and notified the nurses of the patient's death.

No one questioned Evans' demise.

After that killing, something in Harvey awakened; something sinister and monstrous.

After three weeks, another person fell victim to Harvey's hands yet again. This time, it was an elderly woman; the reason behind this particular murder wasn't clear – what was established was the fact that Harvey disconnected the woman's tube to the oxygen tank just when she needed it most. Again, the act was not discovered, driving the orderly to be braver in his following crimes.

Within just a year, he killed 12 people swiftly – no one suspected, no one even doubted the fact that he seemed to be always close to the patient moments before their death. His methods varied – sometimes he used materials, other times he used drugs.

Each time, the murder was more brutal than before. When angered, when bored, and when there were opportunities – these are the moments when Harvey "The Angel of Death" would come.

One time, a patient felt that Harvey was trying to kill him, so he knocked him out with a bedpan. As revenge, the orderly waited until it was night time before he sneaked into the patient's room and inserted a coat hanger into his catheter. The puncture wound created, resulted in an infection which killed the patient just a few days later.

On March 31, 1971, a drunk Harvey was arrested because of burglary and out of the blue, he began "babbling" about the killings he did at the hospital. The officer who received the case took the confessions seriously and investigated the claims; unfortunately, they found no solid evidence to incarcerate the orderly.

In the end, he admitted to the burglary so that the charge could be reduced to petty theft, paid a small fine, and resigned from the hospital to enter the US Air Force.

The plot thickened after that.

Less than a year after enlisting himself in the Air Force, Harvey was discharged for reasons which were not specified in the reports. According to rumors, it seemed like the officers found out about his "confessions" to the police and they didn't want to involve the Force with issues as controversial as those, so he was dismissed.

This "rejection" made Harvey depressed, so much that he even admitted himself to Veteran's Administration Medical Center in July 1972, to curb his inner demons. In August 25, however, he was released even though no positive changes in him occurred.

Several weeks later, he admitted himself once again, and through the course of his confinement, received 21 ECT (electroshock therapy) treatments. In mid-October, he was once again released. Later on, Goldie Harvey, his mother, would give her statement blaming the hospital for releasing her son so soon despite his lack of improvement.

After his release from the hospital, Harvey dedicated the following months to start over. He was able to secure jobs at two different hospitals at the same time; fortunately, his tasks didn't require him to be close to any patient, so his crimes temporarily stopped. After he resigned from the two hospitals, he accepted a job as a telephone operator, then as a clerk in St. Luke's Hospital in Fort Thomas, Kentucky.

Experts say that at this time, Harvey was still "growing";

he wasn't comfortable to kill outside the only safe place he knew – a hospital. It would have been best if he never found another hospital to work at, but that was not the case.

When he went back to Cincinnati, Ohio in September of 1975, he was immediately accepted at V.A. Medical Hospital as a nightshift aid. There, he performed a range of roles, from being a nursing aide, a cardiac catheterization technician, a housekeeping helper, to an assistant to the personnel who did the autopsy routines.

All these roles were pointless because he already knew what his purpose was: to be The Angel of Death. With more tasks on his hands, and with little supervision (since he worked nightshifts), he would be able to fulfill this role without so much suspicion from his colleagues.

For one decade Harvey was able to execute at least 15 people; his "murder weapons" varied, but most of the time, he used arsenic and cyanide (pre-mixed at home) in different fashions – there were times he just added the poison to the patient's drinks, while on other occasions, he opted to inject them in the patient or force it down the IV tubes. When he ran out of arsenic and cyanide, he would use ordinary things like plastic bags (used for choking) and rat poison (sprinkled on dessert).

While doing all these crimes, he was monitoring everything – from his patient's identity, the date he killed them, and the method he used. Not only that, but he also collected books and journals about health and medicine, so that he could "update" his knowledge on possible killing methods, and learn about techniques which could mask his crimes. Over the years, he was known to have accumulated 30 lbs of cyanide!

Reports said he stole little amounts of the poison whenever it was opportune and kept it at home for "safekeeping".

During the 1980s, Harvey's killings took a turn for the worse: he began poisoning people outside the hospital. First, it was his gay lover, Carl Hoeweler, whom he moved in with. Apparently, he suspected that Hoeweler was having an affair with another guy, so he added arsenic into his drink, making him too ill to leave the apartment.

Next were his neighbors, Diane Alexander and Helen Metzger, who got into an argument with him. He laced Alexander's drink with hepatitis serum, but thankfully, she was cured before the infection killed her. Metzger wasn't that fortunate because Harvey used arsenic on her pie, killing her almost instantly.

Harvey also got into a fight with Hoeweler's parents, so he poisoned them little by little, until Hoeweler's father suffered a stroke and was admitted to Providence Hospital.

One day, Harvey visited him and traced his pudding with arsenic; he died later that evening. Hoeweler's mother was luckier, for even though Harvey kept on poisoning her on and off within a year, she survived. Perhaps fed up with Harvey's "ministrations", Hoeweler broke up with him in 1984, and as expected, it angered the serial killer so much that he spent the next two years trying to kill Hoeweler with his deadly concoctions.

While he failed in this mission, he did manage to send Hoeweler to the hospital for a poisonous solution he ingested without his knowledge. When attempts to kill his former lover failed him, Harvey thought of killing one of Hoeweler's female friends, but that too, was unsuccessful.

On July 18, 1985, security guards noticed that Harvey was acting strangely, so they stopped him on his way and demanded to inspect the gym bag he was carrying. Inside, they found a pistol, a cocaine spoon, surgical gloves and scissors, hypodermic needles, two occult books, one book about a serial killer named Charles Sobhraj, and many medical texts.

Despite the fact that all the contents (except the medical texts) were suspicious, he was only fined $50 for carrying a weapon in a federal area. The hospital then asked him to resign quietly WITHOUT putting the said incident in his work records; in fact, they put nothing but good things about him!

As a result, Harvey was able to kill 23 more people in his next employment as a full-time nurses' aide in Cincinnati's Drake Memorial Hospital. He was accepted there 7 months after the quiet resignation, and at first, was only assigned as a part-time nursing aide.

But since they found nothing suspicious about him, and his previous employment only mentioned good things about his work ethics, they gave him a full-time job. He killed using various methods again, by pulling out life support, injecting cyanide, arsenic, and chemical cleansers, as well as injecting air into the clients' veins.

By 1987, Harvey was already known as the Angel of Death, since he seemed to always be around the patients at the time of their deaths, but still, no one suspected that he actually murdered them.

Until John Powell died.

John Powell was formerly a comatose patient, but at the time of his death, he was already recovering. This prompted an autopsy investigation, where the assistant coroner smelled the scent of almonds – a tell-tale sign of cyanide. At first, they suspected Powell's friends and family, but when they found no motive, they concentrated on the hospital staff who had access to the patient's room. After learning that Harvey was the "Angel of Death", they concentrated the investigation on him.

With search warrant on their hands, the police felt that they were closer to the truth. At first, The Angel of Death pleaded not guilty by the virtue of insanity, but soon enough – when the police saw his occult books, medical texts, jars of poisons, and the list which detailed his murders – he struck a deal to avoid Ohio's death penalty.

He admitted to killing 33 people in 17 years, but the numbers grew to 70, which the officers became suspicious about, so they asked his mental state to be examined. The result was on point: Donald Harvey was a competent, sane man, but he killed impulsively because of the tension building in his mind and body.

When asked why he killed, he simply said that it was about control – he was controlled for 18 years, so it was only fair to control other people's lives when he could. The interviewer inquired: "What right did you have to do that?", to which he answered: "After I didn't get caught for the first 15 murders, I decided it was my right, so I played God."

At the end of the trial, Donald "The Angel of Death" Harvey was sentenced with 28 consecutive life terms in Southern Ohio Correctional Facility, plus $270,000 in fines. He is also eligible for parole, but the hearing will be scheduled in 2043; by then, Donald Harvey will be already 95 years old.

In 2001, the Associated Press released an article which listed the worst serial killers the United States ever had; Donald Harvey ranked number one, surpassing the infamous John Wayne Gacy.

Chapter 5: Dennis Nilsen

Perhaps one of the most "prolific" serial killers in Britain-- Dennis Nilsen was arrested due to a blocked toilet bowl. Sounds funny? Well, wait until you hear about the murders he committed. Dennis was able to kill 15 people in the span of 5 years.

Like the previous two cases, Dennis also grew up in a faulty family. He was born on November 23, 1945. He lived with his mother and siblings in his grandfather's home. Dennis adored his grandfather, so when he died when he was only 6 years old, viewing his corpse was traumatizing.

Since the marriage with his father wasn't satisfying, Dennis's mother remarried and gave birth to 4 more children. This left Dennis lonely and disengaged. Growing up, he already recognized his affection for the same sex, but he didn't pursue any of his attraction. When he reached the age of 15, he enrolled in the army where he served as a cook. His primary role there was a butcher-- his skills proved to be useful in the 5 years of his killing spree.

It is also worth mentioning that during his time there, he started to feel attraction to his comrades. He disliked that feeling and resorted to deciding that he was bisexual and not gay. Around this time, Dennis also developed a habit of "turning" himself into a corpse. He would often cover himself with talc and color his lips blue. After that, he would look at a mirror and masturbate while looking at himself.

When his army career came to an end, he became a Corporal and was assigned in Shetland Islands where he fell in love with an 18 year old private. Unfortunately, the young private did not return his love. This made Dennis feel guiltier.

From the army, he decided to train for the police. While training, he discovered a fondness for visiting morgues. Around the time of his service in the Metropolitan Police, he became a frequent visitor of gay bars like The Golden Lion, The Salisbury, and The Black Cap. You may think that he would use being a policeman to his advantage, especially since he would become a serial killer. But no, he resigned and took a job as a recruiter.

Cook, police, and recruitment interviewer-- nothing seemed to be wrong with this man. He was even able to have a sort-of healthy relationship. In 1975, he lived together with David Gallichan in 195 Melrose Avenue. Although David denied any form of homosexual relationship, they co-habited for two years.

They worked on their garden together and even bought a dog to keep them company. When David left him due to falling out of love, Dennis' world spiralled down-- so much that he took the life of his first victim only 18 months after the breakup.

On December 29, 1978, Dennis met his first victim. A child named Steven Holmes, who was at that time only 14 years old. Dennis claimed that he took him from a gay bar, but from other accounts, he lured him into drinking in Melrose Avenue.

Nothing was mentioned if the two had sex that night, but what was clear was Steven tried to leave on the morning of December 30. Not wanting him to go anywhere, Dennis strangled him using a necktie. Then, he proceeded in drowning him in a bucket of water.

He took the corpse into his bathroom to "wash" it, before laying it down on his bed. He tried to have sex with it, but when he was unsuccessful, he resorted to simply sleeping beside it. He even said that the corpse was beautiful. After that, he hid the body under his floorboards for more than seven months before finally burning it.

Almost a year after killing Steven, Dennis set about to kill another man-- this time a student tourist named Kenneth

Ockendon. They met each other in a bar, and went on a sight seeing date. They returned home to Dennis's apartment, but when morning came and Kenneth wanted to leave, Dennis responded by strangling him using an electrical cord until he died.

He took the corpse into the bathroom and washed it before setting it down on the bed. He had sex with it, but more that that, he took photos and slept beside it. When the time was right, he buried the body under the floorboards again, but occasionally he would get it out to converse with it as though it was alive.

Dennis waited 5 months before killing his next victim. That victim was Martyn Duffey, a homeless 16 year old from Merseyside. He was invited into Dennis' apartment for a drink, and again, when he attempted to leave, he was strangled and drowned to death in the kitchen sink.

Again, he brought the body back to bed, masturbated on it and had sex with it. He didn't bury it under the floorboards right away (he simply kept the body in the wardrobe) because he used the body as if it was a living companion. After two weeks, he decided that it was time for Martyn to join Kenneth.

After some time, Dennis thought that he was running out

of space. What he did was horrible, but calculated. He took the two bodies in the bath and dissected them into smaller pieces. He boiled the parts in a large cooking pot before finally keeping them in a suitcase which he bought especially for that use.

When 1981 came, Dennis had already killed 12 people in his apartment, including 27 year old Billy Sutherland, who followed him to his apartment and was considered by Dennis as a "pest". Then, there was 24 year old Malcolm Barlow who was mentally challenged.

Of the 12 victims, only the four mentioned here were identified. When Dennis was interviewed, he mentioned about one victim who was Irish and was heavily tattooed. He recollected that the man was wearing a "Cut Here" tattoo on his neck-- guess what? Dennis obliged to the request.

By the time Dennis killed Malcolm, he was forced to move out of his apartment. This was partly due to his not-so-pleasant relationship with his landlord who thought he was a troublesome tenant. This was because when the other tenants complained of the awful smell, Dennis convinced them that it was the structure of the building itself.

When Dennis' apartment was attacked by burglars and

most of his possessions were destroyed, the landlord seized the opportunity to take him out. He offered Dennis 1000 pounds and directed him to a new apartment in Cranley Gardens.

So, you must be wondering what he did to all the bodies in his apartment. Well, he took different measures to dispose of them. The major manner of disposal was a bonfire-- he performed two. Dennis even had some troubles in locating all the body parts (remember, he butchered his victims before keeping the dismembered bodies in different places of the house), and at one point he even fell because a pair of legs under the cupboard tripped him on the floor.

Some internal organs were put between his fences and walls where they would be eaten by rats and other pests. The bigger limbs were buried in the gardens, and the bones were crushed after the bonfire.

Dennis moved to No. 23 Cranley Gardens in the year 1982 and waited a few months before killing his next prey. He waited that much time probably because of the "inconvenience" brought about by the place. No. 23 had no floorboards, and no gardens, so hiding a body would prove to be a very difficult task. But he could not stifle his impulse to kill, so in March he murdered John Howlett--

a felon. After him, Archibald Graham and Steven Sinclair followed.

As for the manner of disposal, he got more creative. He butchered the body into smaller pieces and boiled them to make them softer. Afterwards, he would flush them down the toilet. This eventually led to his arrest.

The other tenants reported a problem in the drainage so they called Dyno-Rod. Upon inspection, Mike Cattran, the assigned man to deal with the blockage noticed what seemed to be human flesh. He called his supervisor and they said it would be further investigated. The inspection was done together with all the tenants, including Dennis, so he must have had a pretty good prediction of his future arrest. He tried to cover his crimes by removing the flesh in the drain, but one tenant caught him and found his actions suspicious.

The next morning, they investigated again, but the drain cover was placed weirdly and the human flesh was gone, except for human bones. When they called the police, a detective named Peter Jay confirmed that the flesh and the bones came from a human.

So they went about questioning Dennis. At first, Dennis feigned disbelief, but Detective Jay asked him firmly to "stop messing around". He asked him again where the remaining body parts were. Surprisingly, Dennis answered-- "In two plastic bags, in the wardrobe, next door." And he even led the way.

After determining the location of the other body parts, Dennis was arrested. The police asked him if there was just one body, or if there were two-- he answered "15 or 16 since 1978".

After his arrest, Dennis provided detailed information about the murders he committed. Aside from that, he also admitted to seven attempted murders. He showed not a second of remorse or regret-- in fact, he was very enthusiastic in giving details: he told the police about the bodies in 195 Melrose Street.

During his trial, he wrote over 50 notebooks of info about what he did to the victims and he also drew sketches. Although he did not show any form of regret, he had the nerve to have "concern" on how the public would see him. It was clear that Dennis would be convicted-- the authorities just did not know whether it would be murder or manslaughter.

On October 24, 1983 he was convicted for 6 counts of murder and 2 counts of attempted murder. He was sentenced to life imprisonment with no parole for 25 years. Throughout the trial, Dennis' plea was not guilty, all the while insisting that he did it because of insanity. He even said that there were 7 victims whom he let free because he was able to "snap out of it". However, the jury did not side with him: the evidence found was physical, like the photographs, the chopping board, and the cooking pot.

Many psychiatrists tried diagnosing Dennis's condition. But one (Dr. Paul Bowden) concluded that Dennis was "cognizant"-- he was capable of being manipulative, with only a small trace of mental abnormality. While he was in prison, he engaged in some homosexual relationships, one with David Martin (a cross dressing robber), who in the end killed himself.

While serving time, Dennis exerted a lot of efforts in writing journals, poetry, and letters. The topic of course, was himself.

Chapter 6: Donald "Pee Wee" Gaskins

On March 13, 1933, Donald Gaskins was born in Florence County in South Carolina. Even before he was born, things weren't looking up for him. Firstly, his mother was unmarried at the time of his conception, secondly, she had the habit of moving from the company of one man to another and not one of these men treated young Donald Gaskins with care; in fact, they pretty much beat him up for existing. Thirdly, when she did marry, she chose the wrong man who regularly beat not just Donald, but also his 4 step-siblings.

Because of his small frame, Gaskins was called Pee Wee at an early age. The chaos and violence he experienced at home reflected in his school life: often times he would fight with fellow students, both boys and girls, and the teachers often reprimanded him for it. At age 11, he was already a dropout, working instead at a garage and helping at the family farm.

Deep inside, Pee Wee had already harbored a great dislike for people, especially women, so when he met two other boys close to his age who were also out of school, he felt a deep connection with them.

Marsh, Danny, and Pee Wee formed a group called "The Trouble Trio". They spread havoc in the area, bullying kids, vandalizing, stealing, and even raping young boys and threatening them so they wouldn't tell. Their escapades only stopped after they were caught molesting Marsh' younger sister; as a punishment, all boys were bound and beaten by their parents.

Marsh and Danny left the neighborhood right after, leaving Gaskins to perform all the troubles alone. One day in 1946 – when Gaskins was just 13 years old – a girl he knew saw him stealing from a home. The girl tried to stop him with an ax, but young Gaskins was swift: he took the ax by force and hit the girl on her head and arms. Fortunately, she survived and Gaskins was arrested. As a penalty, he was obligated to attend a reform school, South Carolina Industrial School for Boys, until he reached the age of 18.

One of the saddest parts of the court proceedings was the fact that it was only then that Gaskins heard of his full name being spoken, which showed how uncaring his environment was.

But, you see, the problem with reform schools back then was the fact that they didn't encourage reform – they encouraged violence. The minute Gaskins arrived there, he knew that it was going to be a nightmare. And why wouldn't he think that?

Shortly after arriving, a group of 20 boys attacked and raped him; as a result, he spent his time at school either trying to escape other attacks, or gaining the protection of the Boss-Boy, the leader in their dorm. The problem was, to gain that protection, he had to perform sexual favors for the boss. Time and time again, he tried to escape, but each time an attempt failed, he was beaten to a pulp. Then things got worse when the Boss-Boy "allowed" gang members which he favored to also rape Gaskins.

At one point, he was able to escape successfully and married a 13-year old girl he met in a travelling carnival. Out of the blue, Gaskins decided to turn himself in and finish the remaining time he needed to spend in the reform school.

Upon being released on his 18th birthday on March of 1951, he went back to his old ways of brewing trouble: he asked several tobacco farmers to burn their barns for insurance payments. It was rumored that he started the trend, but the claim was never investigated since he was sent to prison anyway after he killed a girl who allegedly accused him of starting the fires. The crime was brutal: with a hammer in hand, he pounded it onto the girl's head so hard that it split her skull.

Gaskins received a 5-year sentence for his crime, and this time, even though he was going to be in a real prison, he knew what to do. First, he performed sexual favors in exchange for protection, then he worked to be one of the "Power Men" – those inmates who couldn't be touched because of their brutality. Gaskins knew that people wouldn't find him particularly intimidating because of his small frame, so he needed to prove it through his actions.

He thought that killing someone would do the job – so he did.

First, he gained the trust of the intimidating inmate named Hazel Brazell, then, when an opportune time presented itself, he slit his throat. Sure, Gaskins was punished with an additional three years in prison for the murder, but he knew that those years would be lighter – he was a Power Man so people would now think twice before attacking him.

In 1955, however, bad news reached him: his wife filed for divorce. Clearly, this angered Gaskins for he was able to summon the courage to escape successfully from prison. He found another travelling carnival, met a woman, and married her although their marriage only lasted for half a month.

After that, he got involved with another woman, who, unknown to him only used him to free her "brother". In the end, he found out that the duo tricked him – the "brother" was really the husband and after bailing him out, they left Gaskins alone and without a car.

The police recognized Gaskins from when he bailed the "brother" out, so he was arrested again and was sentenced with an additional 9 months in jail.

In 1961, Gaskins was released from prison and worked in a tobacco farm in Florence, South Carolina; after that he worked for a traveling minister as a driver and assistant. He saw this as an opportunity to burglarize homes: as the ministry traveled, he sneaked into homes and stole things. Because the crimes were "scattered", the police had a hard time tracing the culprit.

A year later, Gaskins married for the third time, but it didn't stop him from committing heinous crimes, including raping a 12-year-old girl for which he was arrested. Gaskins escaped and before long, he found another girl, a 17-year-old one, whom he also raped. That girl turned him in to the authorities, who sentenced him to six years in prison. He was paroled in 1968 – after stepping out of jail, he vowed never to return there.

Throughout the years, Gaskins never showed that he would someday become a serial killer. True, he was capable of murdering people, but each time he did so, it seemed like he had a reason: either he was angry, he was threatened, or he was insulted – not once did he show any sign of wanting to kill frequently. But as it was, there's always a "wakeup call".

The wakeup call happened in September of 1969; Gaskins

offered a ride to a young hitchhiker girl and then he proposed that the two of them have sex. When the girl laughed, Gaskins went wild: he knocked the girl unconscious, raped and sodomized her, and then weighed her down to drown in a swamp. After that, Gaskin realized how satisfying it was to kill; he said it satisfies the old, aggravating, and bothersome feelings that he had.

Later on, he would reveal that at times, he also ate some of his victims.

First of all, one must understand that Gaskins divided his killings into two categories: the "recreational" and the "serious" ones. He was dismissive about his recreational murders because the method was so simple: wait until it was weekend, pick up someone from the highway (mostly hitchhikers), rape them, and then torture them to death. By 1975, he had already killed at least 80 boys and girls.

His serious murders were more momentous because the victims were people he personally knew. In 1970, for example, he killed his niece, Janice Kirby, 15 and her friend, Patricia Alsobrook. The two just left the bar and were promised by Gaskins a ride home; instead of fulfilling his promise, he drove them to an abandoned place, then proceeded to rape and torture them without hesitation. After the crime, he drowned them in two different locations.

Martha Dicks, an African American girl, became Gaskins

second serious murder. The twenty-year-old knew of Gaskins in a car repair shop he once worked at; according to reports, Dicks had a crush on him and would often follow him around while working.

Perhaps one of the most notable serious murders Gaskins committed was the murder of a mother and her two-year-old daughter. Doreen Dempsey was just 23 years old at that time, without a husband to care for her and her baby girl; looking to have a better life, she decided to move away from the area and accepted a ride from her friend, Gaskins.

She didn't know that that decision would cost her everything. Instead of dropping them to the bus station as what was originally planned, Gaskins brought them to a wooded area, raped the mother and child, killed them, and then buried them both. More horrifying was the fact that Doreen was pregnant when the crime happened.

In an interview later on, Gaskins admitted that raping the two-year-old was one of the best experiences he had.

Many investigators said that one of the factors why Gaskins became a successful serial killer despite the intensity and frequency of his murders, was his independence: he would pickup his victims alone, he raped, tortured, and killed them alone, and he also didn't ask for help in burying.

Well, that changed when he killed three people all at the same time in 1975. Reports said the three were not runaways, nor were they hitchhikers; they owned a van but it broke down on the highway where, unfortunately, Gaskins was waiting for his next "catch". Knowing how hard it would be to accomplish the task of disposing three people with a vehicle, he contacted Walter Neely, an ex-convict, for assistance. Neely drove the van to Gaskin's home, so that he could repaint and sell it.

His second error happened when he accepted a job as a hired killer. Due to this, more people knew of his capability to kill.

His third mistake occurred when he disclosed the whereabouts of the graves of the people he murdered to Walter Neely.

Kim Ghelkins was just a 13-year-old girl when she disappeared. The investigation happened quickly and when it was discovered that Gaskins made a pass on the girl and she refused, his apartment was searched, revealing clothes which belonged to the Ghelkins. Right then and there the police knew that they had to search all angles that may give Gaskins away.

So they pressured Walter Neely, Gaskin's known friend, to reveal all the things he knew about his confidante.

Neely didn't disappoint: he showed them Gaskins' personal graveyard.

The trial was long and stressful, not just for the prosecutors, but also for Gaskins since the death penalty was enforced in South Carolina and he knew that his chances of staying alive were slim to none. True enough, the jury decided that his crimes were so horrendous he had to pay with his life. On September 6, 1991, Donald "Pee Wee" Gaskins was executed in the electric chair.

Chapter 7: Dr. Harold Frederick Shipman

You couldn't discuss serial killers without mentioning and delving deeper into the mind of Harold Shipman. Not only did he kill using his medical degree, he also showed no qualms in murdering his patients, in fact, it was as if he found it pleasant each time he killed. What could possibly drive Dr. Shipman into murdering at least 215 people?

Harold Frederick Shipman, Fred to his family, was the second child of an ordinary family who lived in Nottingham. He was born on January 14, 1946. He was the favorite of his Mother, Vera, who taught him that he was superior above others.

Due to his closeness to his mother, Fred took care of her the minute she was diagnosed with lung cancer. While attending to her, Fred saw how morphine was able to help ease the pain. However, when Vera finally succumbed to the disease, Fred was devastated. He became determined to become a doctor, so he enrolled in Leeds University. At first, he failed the entrance exam, but on the second time, he succeeded. From there, he started his internship in hospitals.

When he was 19, he met Primrose, who became his wife. By the year 1974, Fred was already a father of two children. In that year, too, he became a doctor who specialized in family practice in Abraham Ormerod Medical Centre in Todmorden, West Yorkshire. At first, everything went smoothly, until Fred became addicted to the painkiller Pethidine.

Because of his addiction to the drug, he made prescriptions of it in huge doses. When caught in 1975, he was fined with a small amount of 600 pounds, and was punished for forgery.

In 1977, it seemed like Fred found his niche in Donneybrook Medical Center. He became a hard working doctor, and a good colleague and was able to stay there for almost 2 decades. Although he became unnecessarily mean to junior staff, his reputation was overall good.

That was until someone noticed that there was an increase in the death toll in patients under Dr. Shipman's care.

Another doctor also thought that the "victims" died while assuming the same pose-- they were all fully clothed, and were either sitting up, or reclining. He approached Fred about it, but the doctor told him there was no need to worry. Another colleague of his, Dr. Susan Booth noticed the patients' poses so the police was brought in. In the silent investigation, nothing amiss was found. All of Fred's records were good, but they failed to learn about his previous case with the pethidine addiction. It would be revealed later that Fred was falsifying the records of his patients to make certain that the cause of death would coincide with the patients' history.

With his luck, Fred continued to practice his profession. He often attended to the elderly who wanted their doctor to check up on them in their own homes. All his luck, however, ran out when he killed a patient with a very determined daughter.

The patient that put a stop to his serial killing was Kathleen Grundy. Despite her age, which was 81, Kathleen was a healthy patient. But on June 24, 1998, she was found dead in her home shortly after Fred made a home visit.

Kathleen's daughter, Angela Woodruff, was advised by Fred that there was no need for an autopsy. Since she thought nothing ill of the doctor, she didn't proceed with the autopsy, but she had her mother buried instead of cremated-- which was against Fred's advice. Apparently, to get rid of all evidence, Fred often advised the families of his patients to have their bodies cremated.

Angela was very active in taking care of her mother, including her legal affairs, so imagine her surprise when she found out that Kathleen made another will. In the new will, Kathleen was leaving a large sum of money under Dr. Shipman's name. Suspicious, Angela contacted the police, which promptly ordered to exhume Kathleen's body.

Upon examination of the body, it was revealed that Kathleen died of a morphine overdose, which was administered three hours before her death. From there the police tracked down other patients of Dr. Shipman who died and were buried instead of cremated.

Fred was arrested and tried in Preston Crown Court on October 5, 1999. He was charged with only 15 counts of murder on January 31, 2000. Throughout the investigation, the police found a lot of evidence against him.

Post mortem findings of his patients reported morphine toxicity. The new will by Kathleen Grundy was also examined for her fingerprints. Result showed it was never handled by her. The handwriting expert also stated that her signature was forged. A computer analyst was also summoned. He told the police about the changes that Fred made to the records of his patients.

He often did it when families became suspicious of the cause of death, especially when the patients had no signs of what Fred was mentioning. Another gruesome piece of evidence was phone records. Apparently, when a patient was dying in front of the family, Fred would call the emergency service, and then he would cancel the service once the patient was dead.

The evidence was this: there were really no calls placed. And lastly, there was evidence that showed how he prescribed morphine to patients who didn't need it, and how he upped the doses to those who did. Families even reported that even after the death of the patient, Fred would visit their home to collect and dispose "supplies".

At first, the defence tried to argue that no one actually saw Fred kill any of his patients, and that the morphine overdose was out of compassion to free the patients from pain. The jury didn't agree with them largely due to the evidence found, and the fact that most of his patients were not terminally ill, hence they didn't need to be freed from pain.

Chapter 8: Pedro Alonso Lopez

Pedro Alonso Lopez was one of the most prolific serials killers, especially in South America. Although he was charged with 110 counts of murder, he confessed to committing over 300 killings.

Born in Tolmia Columbia in the year 1949, Pedro Alonzo Lopez had 13 siblings to a prostitute mother. When he was 8 years old, he was already caught molesting his younger sister. This prompted his family to kick him out. In the streets a man found him. He temporarily took him home, but while under his wing, he sodomized Pedro. Afterwards he also kicked him out. On the streets, he became paranoid of strangers. He would wait until it was night before searching for food, and in the daylight, he would hide.

Fortunately, when he reached Bogota (he was already 12), an American couple adopted him. He was given a room, and was even enrolled in school. Despite the good life he had with the couple, he still stole money from his school and left. According to Pedro, a school teacher molested him.

After he took off, he lived on the streets again-- surviving while stealing cars and selling them to chop shops. At 18, he was caught and was sentenced to 7 years in prison. In prison, he was gang raped by 4 men, all of whom he killed with a knife. Since it was an act of self-defense, the police only added 2 years to his sentence. He was finally released in 1978.

Although it wasn't a sure notion, it was highly believed that it was his time in prison that drove him to have fear and anger towards girls. So, after he was granted freedom, he travelled all around Peru, but not to have a better life. Instead he took girls from various Indian tribes and raped and killed them.

He was caught in the act of kidnapping a 9 year old girl, so the tribe, Ayacuchos, decided to bury him alive. The sand was already up to his neck when an American found what was going on stopped the punishment and convinced them to turn him over to Peruvian authorities.

Unfortunately, the authorities thought that transporting him to Ecuador was enough of a punishment. This might be because the act of kidnapping was not culminated, and there was no evidence of the murders he said he committed to 100 girls.

While in Ecuador, he did the same exploration as he did in Peru. He kidnapped young girls, raped, and killed them. Although sudden and consecutive disappearances were noticed, the authorities simply thought it was a part of the already existing sex slave dilemma.

When a flash-flood happened in 1980, 4 bodies of young girls were uncovered. No reports about the cause of death were released but it was very clear that foul play was involved. Shortly after that, Pedro was, again, caught in the act of kidnapping a girl. Carvina Poveda was innocently shopping when she noticed that Pedro was forcibly taking her 12 year old daughter. The police took Pedro into custody and immediately asked about his crime, the problem was, Pedro wasn't cooperative.

They rectified this situation by dressing a priest with prison clothes. He was then put into Pedro's cell. From there, Pedro's confession was a breeze.

The contents of his confessions, however, were gruesome and would very much prove that he had lost grip on his life at some point.

He said that he murdered 100 girls in Peru, 100 in Ecuador, and 100 in Columbia. His tactic would be to approach them at day, often times, where there were crowds. Pedro said it made the victims feel more secure. While talking to them, he would talk sweetly, telling them that he had gifts for them or for their mother. There were times when he would "investigate" first for two to three days. He would learn about the routine of the victim and the mother so that he would know when to strike.

The crime scene had to be ready even before the kidnapping, because that made everything easy. Sometimes the victims would be the only one in the setup, but most of the time, she would join others. Pedro never killed while it was dark because it was very important for him to see the life leave the girls' eyes when he was strangling them to death.

The reason why he buried the bodies together was because he did not want them to be lonely-- he would even have "tea parties" with them. But after a while, he would get bored, so another child would be added. Pedro also said that he treated them as friends, but only after they died. Even after a victim's death, Pedro would still rape the body.

His story was so unbelievable that the police questioned its veracity, Pedro seemed offended with this so he took the police to places where he buried the children. 53 bodies were recovered, but the other 28 places were empty. However, authorities said it could be because of flash floods, and scavenging animals.

In the end he was sentenced to be imprisoned. You might think that he would serve lifetime in confinement, but no. He was released in 1998 after 20 years. Back then, Ecuador had no death penalties, so he was simply released and deported to Columbia as he no longer had the visa to Ecuador. Others believed him to be already dead, especially with all the bounties on his head.

What made Pedro fearsome was the way he enjoyed killing girls. He had this "criteria" in his head as to who his victims would be. In an interview, he said that the girl's face should be sweet and innocent. She should be helpful to her mother in doing chores. A trinket should be offered to her, most commonly a hand mirror. He would lure them to the end of the town with a promise of another trinket for her mother.

He cuddled with them before raping them, and when the first morning light appeared, he would feel "excited". There was no use killing them in the dark because he couldn't see their eyes.

Some of the things he told Ron Laytner from the National Examiner were bone chilling. He said "It would take 15 minutes for them to die... I was very considerate; I always made sure they were dead. Sometimes I even kill them all over again." As for the murders, he stated: "The moment of death is enthralling and exciting. Only those who actually kill know what I mean. When I am released, I will feel that moment again. "

Conclusion

Thank you again for purchasing this book!

I hope these stories of horrible murders and crime intrigued you and I hope you may have learned a lesson when it comes to trusting strangers and letting your children meander on their own. The chances that you are living near the abode of a serial killer could be very low, but it never hurts to be more careful.

Could I please ask you one small favour? If you enjoyed this book, could you be so kind as to give me a review? It helps me so much, so I thank you in advance!

Check Out My Other Books

Below you'll find some of my other popular books that are popular on Amazon and Kindle as well. You can visit my author page on Amazon to see other work done by me. (Seth Balfour).

True Ghost Stories

UFOs And Aliens

Conspiracy Theories

Missing People

Serial Killers

Cannibal Killers

Missing People – Volume 2

Unexplained Disappearances

Cold Cases True Crime

Haunted Asylums

Haunted Asylums – Volume 2

True Ghost Stories – Volume 2

Women Who Kill

You can simply search for these titles on the Amazon website with my name to find them.

Want more books?

Would you love books delivered straight to your inbox every week?

Free?

How about non-fiction books on all kinds of subjects?

We send out e-books to our loyal subscribers every week to download and enjoy!

All you have to do is join! It's so easy!

Just visit the link below to sign up and then wait for your books to arrive!

www.LibraryBugs.com

Enjoy :)